WHO AM I?

An exploration of our essential nature

B E Mayne

WHO AM I?

An Exploration of Our Essential Nature

Cover illustration: Shutterstock

Layout: Christian Paaske

bemayne@gmail.com

What is the use of knowing about everything else when you do not yet know Who you are? Self-inquiry is the one infallible means, the only direct one, of realizing the unconditioned, absolute Being you really are.

Ramana Maharshi

Contents

Introduction

How to use this

Congratulations!

Just a few ever wonder who they really are, even fewer seriously explore the topic, and only the rarest manages the direct experience of realizing the core self.

Although becoming conscious of it is a rare attainment, this core self is accessible to all and naturally part of what we each are as human beings. It is not a hidden secret but an obvious aspect of ourselves we pay no attention to. This is largely because our senses and mind are constantly drawn away from it and prefer to identify with being an acquired artificial construct we call our personality and ego which is what is constantly caught up in seeking from or reacting to what is external.

These notes could be called '*Spirituality 101*', or '*Non-duality/Advaita Made Simple*', because they offer a step-by-step explanation of why we are not who we think we are – leaving who we are as what remains.

Part 1 peels away what we are not to reveal what we are.

Part 2 discusses the implications of this, what our essential qualities are and notes some ways we can realize this 'who I am'.

Part 3 restates who we are with further illustrations and goes on to speak of living life with and without this self.

Part 4 confirms the above findings with quotes from some of the most respected traditions and teachers throughout history.

Accordingly, only Parts 1 and 2 are necessary to discover the answer to the question in the title. It is an answer of such simplicity that it will leave most individual's conceptual thinking unsatisfied and bemused. The reason for this is that conceptual thinking is of the mind, and we need to transcend the mind to experience our real selves.

Could union with reality be equated to being conscious of the peace that is the deep dreamless sleep state when we are not aware of the body or of anything else external whatsoever?

Could it be the state a foetus in the womb is in?

Could it even be what we are preceding the state in the womb?

And if these are true, what are their implications as to the reality of our normal waking state?

For these reasons, Parts 3 and 4 have been added to help bring the message home.

However, as noted, conceptual comprehension of the explanation here will never be enough, because one is still operating in the mind. It is a conscious direct experience of one's state outside of the mind which will bring this truth home.

A summary presentation of Parts 1 and 2 was given to the European membership of Intertel, a high IQ society. It offers a quick overview of the key message. It can be seen with voice accompaniment here: https://www.youtube.com/watch?v=J_6DFIJfR4g

What this is about

This document is not about someone else, but about you, the reader or listener.

You may understand and think about what is said here in a conceptual sense, but *it will only have value if it becomes your own direct experience*.

Situation:
- People believe they are human beings, mind-body complexes, who were born and will die.

Complications:
- Bodies are DNA-based – from parents/ancestry – and everything physical has a limited life span.
- What we consider to be our minds, intellect, personalities/egos and information about the world, our physical selves and our likes and dislikes are acquired externally via senses, modelling, parents, education, society, etc.
- This 'who I think I am', or 'my' body-mind complex, in the waking parts of my life is still with 'me' in a modified form

during the dream parts but disappears entirely during the deep dreamless sleep times.

Questions:
- Who was it that was there in the mind's beginning to learn all that it knows?
- What is my real identity – the one who is with me consistently through my waking, dreaming and deep sleep stages?
- How can I realize this real identity – that which does not change as the human one does through the three states of waking, dreaming and deep sleep?
- What are the implications of such a consistent self?
- Did it really begin with the birth of a body and will it end with that body's death?

Part 1

Who Am I?

Who I believe I am is based on information external to me

Physical Body

Others, usually my parents, have informed me about my birth, that I am human, their child with their DNA, their family name and that my body is ('I' am) of their race(s) and culture(s).

Despite no memory of being born, I soon see and sense there is a body with which I am associated and am told/learn about its physical attributes.

My senses together with others' treatment of me inform me that my body is ('I' am) an individual, separate from others, who have their own bodies.

My parents have given a first name to my body, and I learn to associate it with whom I identify as being.

Although I may suffer the loss or paralysis of some parts of my body, that does not change my still being present and self-aware.

Mind or Subtle Body

I have a mind which is fed by the physical senses of my body (sight, hearing, taste, smell, and touch) and which believes in these sensory perceptions.

My mind is parentally, educationally, and socially conditioned.

I learn and am taught about myself including about my body, my family, culture, nationality and usually about which religion I am expected to follow.

Based on my learning and conditioning, my mind forms my personality and ego, full of likes and dislikes and I act and react accordingly to perceptions of external stimuli, moving toward what I desire and away from what I wish to avoid.

My mind, personality and ego expresses itself through actions using the body's parts (hands, feet, mouth, genitals and organs of excretion).

An important aspect of my mind is the intellect through which I can discriminate about my incoming perceptions, thoughts and outgoing actions.

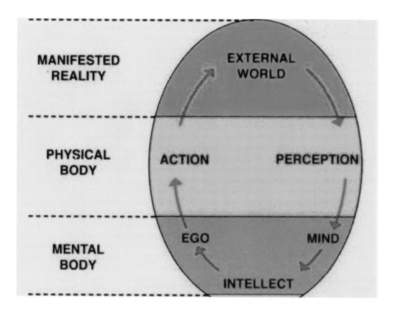

The whole of my mind, or subtle body, with its various parts, seems to act as a functioning unit creating my waking and dreaming worlds and all my associations, actions and reactions to external and mental stimuli.[1]

---

[1] Vedic teachings use the word 'Antahkarana', or 'inner mind', to describe the seat of the mind/subtle body, the subtle source from which it originates.

Causal Body (Absence of Knowledge)

The term 'causal body' is used in Vedic literature to describe a state
we may often encounter in meditation/dhyana or transit through
when surrendering ourselves to sleep. In it, our senses and mind
have been closed down and we cease being aware of the physical
body.

As our mind has become absent, it could be said we are in a state of
forgetfulness, of no knowledge and of emptiness. When we reach
this state, we have **mostly** absorbed ourselves back from
identification with the physical and mental. However, as the
absorption is not complete, Hindu teachings tell us this state is
known as the idea or seed from which the subtle/mental and
physical bodies emerge, hence the name 'causal'. Any remaining
waves of desire or attachment which may still be present in embryo
could sprout, disturbing the peace of full absorption and resulting in
the other two bodies (mental and physical) re-emerging.

What is interesting about the state is that a knowingness remains,
albeit one without having any thought or object of knowledge.
Although it is close to the bliss of deep sleep, we are not unconscious
to it.

Could this most pleasant and peaceful state, virtually empty of body,
senses, mind, thoughts, objects and all knowledge whatsoever be
who we are?

After some period of contemplating it, we realize that it, too, like the physical and subtle bodies, must be objective because ***there is a witness to it.***

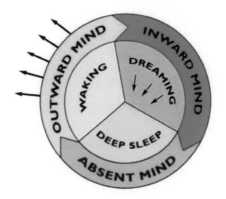

My daily experience informs me my human self goes through 3 states

Waking consciousness in which I am 'the Waker', and my mind, senses and actions focus outwards.

Dreaming sleep in which I am 'the Dreamer', and my mind and awareness focus inwards.

Deep dreamless sleep, when I am 'the Sleeper', at which times my mind does not function at all and I am not even aware of my physical body – this means that if I were my body-mind complex, my life would stop each time I enter deep sleep and start each time I dream or wake up. If so, who is it who remains during deep sleep?[2]

[2] "The senses have separate origin in their several objects. They may be active, as in the waking state, or they may be inactive, as in sleep. He who knows them to be distinct from the changeless Self grieves no more" - **Katha Upanishad 2:3:6**

Who I am must be the subject 'me' rather than an object

My authentic self must be the innermost 'me', 'me' at source, rather than anything considered to be external to it, which would therefore either be separate from this 'me' or extended or reflected aspects of 'me'.

Since I observe and feel my body, it is one with my real identity while I am aware of it, but this is in a transitory way, much like a passing cloud is temporarily one with the sky.

Similarly, I witness my mind and its thoughts, but these are part of me only to the extent my attention focuses on them.

Who am I, if not the body or mind that I am witnessing?[3]

Who is this aware witness?

---

[3] "Know the Self to be sitting in the chariot, the body to be the chariot, the intellect (*buddhi*) the charioteer, and the mind the reins. The senses they call the horses, the objects of the senses their roads. When he (the Highest Self) is in union with the body, the senses, and the mind, then wise people call him the Enjoyer." **Katha Upanishad 3.3**

Clues about who I am from different teachers
– some world famous and others less well known

Neither mind nor body
Turiya is described as the fourth state and is also referred to as samadhi and union.[4] It is likened to being conscious during the deep sleep state – which is when one is beyond both mind and body. This means it must be other than mind and body – and not unconscious as we seem to be in deep sleep.

Being established in an unchanging state senior to time and space
When a weeping disciple begged his master, whose physical body was nearing death, not to leave his students, the master replied, 'Where can I go?', implying he was already established in an unchanging reality.[5]

Another teacher occasionally ended his talks by wishing his audiences a happy stay on earth, suggesting that where he was speaking from is not in this material realm[6] and that our time in this realm is temporary.[7]

A further teacher told a student, 'I am not here now' and, when drinking water, said to another student, 'I am not drinking water. I have never drunk water'. When told someone had come for his blessing but left because he was asleep, this same teacher said the other needn't have gone without the blessing because 'I never sleep' and went out and blessed the one who had come before.[8]

Living as a witness in the world

A Zen master spoke of the world as a hologram on our senses.[9] A hologram is a three-dimensional image made by interference of beams from a coherent light source. This could be heard as another way of saying the world and all the rest of manifested reality can be likened to an illusion projected by a 'light' source from within us and reflected on our senses. Who we are must be the unchanging reality behind the senses, witnessing the illusion/maya, or 'relative reality' of changing manifested creation.

Being oneness

An Indian guru said that when he looked at other people all he saw was 'me'. Another time, he greeted a leader of another religion with the words, 'We come from the same source'. He also spoke of the vision of oneness.[10] An Indian lady, widely considered to be a saint, said that other people were no different than limbs of her own body.[11] That state of oneness must be where such masters are established.[12]

Being 'space'

The same Indian guru and another teacher from England[13] said, 'Become the space'. Such space must be pure, without the distinction of subject and objects.

Being non-personal awareness

Proper dhyana and meditation are considered to be states, rather than practices (an activity or a 'doing' and 'becoming' journey), and a Western teacher commented, 'Meditation is awareness.'[14]

Some quotes from Ramana Maharshi

"Sense-perceptions can only be indirect knowledge, and not direct knowledge. Only one's own awareness is direct knowledge."

"A man does not have to go and find where his eyes are in order to see. The heart is there, always open to you, if you care to enter it, always supporting your movements, although you may be unaware of it. It is perhaps more correct to say that the Self is the Heart. Really the Self is the centre and is everywhere aware of itself as the Heart or Self-awareness."

"The mind of one meditating on a single object becomes one-pointed. And one-pointedness of mind leads to abidance in the self. Real attainment is to be fully conscious, to be aware of surroundings and the people around, to move among them all, but not to merge consciousness in the environment. One should remain in inner independent awareness."

"Awareness is another name for you. Since you are awareness there is no need to attain or cultivate it. All that you have to do is to give up being aware of other things, that is of the not-Self. If one gives up being aware of them then pure awareness alone remains, and that is the Self."

"If you observe awareness steadily, this awareness itself becomes the Guru that will reveal the Truth."

Question: Does my realization help others?
Ramana Maharshi: Yes, certainly! Realization of the Self is the greatest help that can be rendered to humanity. Therefore the saints are said to be helpful, though they remain in forests.
Question: Would it not be better if he mixed with others?
Ramana Maharshi: There are no others to mix with.

_____

Awareness does not belong to an individual person. It is rather an all-inclusive awareness, an unlimited and intelligent eternal oneness alive to itself . . . outside of the material dimensions of time and space.

This pure awareness could also be likened to what real love means. Such love is freely accessible to any person and is not of the time and space of this world. It is therefore not restricted to being about belonging to any form for – or from – any other form.

[4] "7. *Turīya* is not that which is conscious of the internal (subjective) world, nor that which is conscious of the external (objective) world, nor that which is conscious of both, nor that which is a mass all sentiency, nor that which is simple consciousness, nor that which is insentient. (It is) unseen (by any sense organ), not related to anything, incomprehensible (by the mind), uninferable, unthinkable, indescribable, essentially of the nature of Consciousness constituting the Self alone, negation of all phenomena, the Peaceful, all Bliss and the Non-dual. This is what is known as the fourth (*Turīya*). This is the *Ātman* and it has to be realised." **Mandukya Upanishad, verse 7, Swami Nikhilananda (Wisdom Library)**

[5] Ramana Maharshi

[6] *"My kingdom is not of this world."* **New Testament, John 18:36 (KJV)**

[7] Srinivas Arka

[8] Swami Shyam

[9] Robert Aitken Roshi

[10] Swami Shyam

[11] Anandamayi Ma

[12] *A Course in Miracles* speaks of Jesus becoming Christ through being one with God and, rather than seeing the illusion of forms, seeing the face of Christ in all others. *A Course in Miracles*, **Manual for Teachers**, Clarification of Terms 5.2.

[13] Shaun de Warren

[14] Shaun de Warren

Beginnings and endings

– what has a beginning always has an ending.

Anything in the dimensions of time, or activity, and space, or form, is subject to change – everything material or physical.

Is who I am in time? Does who I am have a physical form?

Ego fears death – but is there a part of who we are that has never witnessed birth or death?

Body and mind have beginnings – DNA and the mind's learning and conditioning come to us from others, from outside.

Did our awareness come to us through the birth of a body or was aware intelligence before and underlying the formation of the body and all its DNA?

What precedes birth and even the formation of the body?

The awareness, or creative life power, we are at source must precede and underlie the mind. It could never have been produced through birth – not by DNA nor by the developing mind . . . and nor has it ever been restricted to belonging to any separate individual.

Awareness not only preceded birth but it continues present through all three stages of human lives – waking, dreaming and deep sleep. It lives in the eternal – is timeless.

Who I am must have preceded my having a body and mind

The physical body was not responsible for my awareness. A body could only have been created by a pre-existing intelligence, or intelligent awareness.

An infant's intelligent awareness had to be there for it to be able to learn its name and everything else about it. Babies are surprised to find their hands and feet 'belong' to them. The fact that the name seems foreign to who an infant knows it is at an early age is evidenced by them often referring to their named selves in the third person.

Our intelligent awareness never took birth as a limited human being but had to have already been present in the womb and even prior to the womb ... otherwise wherever else could it have originated from?

This awareness is in the timeless. We see or hear these words with the same awareness we saw or heard with as infants. What is usually referred to as memory is recalling previous experiences of this constant awareness – a constant awareness existing outside of time.

Waking to this awareness is an actual direct experience of coming home to who we already are and have always been. In realizing this, some may even recognize it as a familiar state, one we knew in earliest infancy, for newborn infants – still with no sense that they are human beings with bodies – are still in that state.[15]

See the following simplified diagram showing the three bodies, from the seed of the causal through the mental/subtle to the physical and its relationship to what it considers to be external reality, the mirage or illusion of maya – an ever-changing reflection of imagination on the part of the 'light' of the timeless formless reality of pure awareness.

Note the Vedic separation of the subtle /mental body (*chitta*) into 3 aspects: the mind (*manas*) that receives sensory inputs from the external, the intellect (*buddhi*) which discerns and makes decisions about such incoming stimuli – as well as about thoughts and attention – and the ego (*ahamkara*) which acts and reacts back into the world.[16]

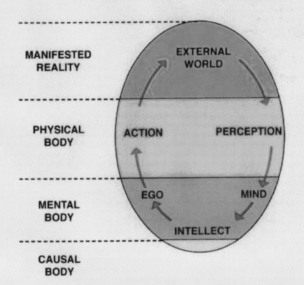

PURE REALITY - AWARENESS

MANIFESTED REALITY

PHYSICAL BODY

MENTAL BODY

CAUSAL BODY

EXTERNAL WORLD

ACTION

PERCEPTION

EGO

MIND

INTELLECT

MAYA - ILLUSION - IMAGINATION

Levels of Perception from the Physical to Pure Awareness

The world will appear different according to the level it is perceived from. Seeing from Reality is dramatically different than seeing from the mind's 'eye'.[17] Accordingly, some teachings speak of opening and using a third or even fourth 'eye'.

Perception through any and all of the physical senses can be done from these levels. Similarly, awareness of thoughts and emotions can also be done from pure awareness rather than from the mind.

Not only is perception of the 'outside' by the 'inside', but the 'inside' is responsible for superimposing what it perceives on the 'outside' – hence perception and perceived are not truly distinct.

We are akin to being the surface of a mirror and our external worlds are the changing reflections on it . . . and we are the ones projecting those reflections back to ourselves.

Buddhists tell us our worlds are projected 'out there' by us. *A Course in Miracles* and other teachings speak of our worlds changing as our own beliefs and perceptions change.

This same pure awareness is also the witness to the seemingly empty causal body.

So, everything is within the sphere of pure awareness, but pure awareness is senior and cannot itself be witnessed by anything within it.

---

[15] We should be as very strangers to the thoughts, customs, and opinions of men in the world, as if we were but little children. So those things would appear to us only which do to children when they are first born. Thomas Traherne

[16] Beyond the senses is the mind, beyond the mind is the intellect, higher than the intellect is the Great Atman [the totality of all minds], higher than the Great Atman is the Unmanifest. Beyond the Unmanifest is the Person, all-pervading, and imperceptible.
- **Katha Upanishad 2.3.7-8**

[17] This is reflected in the title of a book of talks by Gurdjieff, **Views From the Real World**, which implies that where we are looking from makes a difference to our perception.

Part 2

Implications, Qualities and Realization

Implications of who I am

What is at source for me?

The subject/source for all objects and even for itself is my awareness, an intelligence alive to itself which can experience everything, but not itself be experienced by anything external to it.

This could be called conscious awareness (or 'soul' in some religions and the '*atma*' in the Hindu religion – when speaking of an individual's essence, though often intended to mean much more than individual – the oneness of the unlimited and eternal Divine itself).

Qualities

- Eternal – not only timeless, but outside of time

- Formless – outside of spatial dimension

- Unchanging – no activity

What this means

What we know with our minds as the waking state is more a relative, rather than an absolute, reality.

Re-engaging in the waking state, as we do whenever we wake from sleep, and re-identifying with our mind – with its acquired personality and ego – can actually be likened to falling into a 'sleep' or transient dreamworld, something of a state of trance or amnesia in which we have lost sight of who we really are.

What we consider to be ourselves, the world and all manifested creation can be likened to a transitory imagination – what Vedic literature refers to as maya or illusion.

The mind – fed by senses – only recognizes forms, names, and what is visible, finite and changing, while the reality of our essential self is formless, nameless, invisible, infinite and changeless.

What we perceive with the senses is actually our imagined projection, or maya/illusion[18], while that which we cannot perceive with the senses is the truer reality, True Knowledge or *Brahman*.[19]

What has happened, is happening and will happen in the world and to us is not ultimate reality. Because we are eternal and unchanging, it is what has NOT happened and NEVER can happen which is real.

Who we really are never was born and therefore never can die.[20]

[18] **A Course in Miracles** confirms that the world and whatever else we perceive with the senses is illusion. **A Course in Miracles, Manual for Teachers,** Clarification of Terms 4.1 and 2.

[19] Chapter 6, **The Master Key to Self-Realization, Siddharameshwar Maharaj**

[20] *"Jesus said: When you see someone not born from a woman, prostrate yourselves and worship him; he is your Father."* **Gospel of Thomas, saying 15, translation by Stevan Davies**

Realizing Myself as Pure Awareness

The mind, which is the higher part, and receptor, of our senses may hear this message – about the awareness which is prior, and senior, to it – conceptually but is unable to be the reality of what this means, what its experiential implications are.

However, if these qualities are true, such as being eternal, then who I am was also present before my body's birth and will still be there after my body's death.[21] Moreover, it means it is also the underlying reality throughout all of my existence in the 3 states – waking, dreaming, and deep sleep – experienced as a human being.

It is not something to attain, as it is already my essence.[22]

It is to be realized, in the sense of being rediscovered as my living reality.

Realizing it is literally what the term self-realization means. It is also called enlightenment, which is letting go the 'endarkenment' of the mind's beliefs/vasanas/maya/ignorance/false identity

It means relinquishing my mind and personhood as my main identity.[23] My mind cannot be conscious of reality, my true identity. "The greatest barrier to consciousness is the belief that one is already conscious."[24]

If it is formless, it has no boundaries and would therefore be a state of oneness, the union meant by the word yoga. Oneness means an end to duality of all subject and object relationships and the cessation of manifested reality – the world, the solar system and the universe – as existing separate from it.

Being such a state before creation also means one's primary identity is pure awareness, rather than believing one is the consciousness and unconsciousness associated with the human mental states of waking, dreaming and deep sleep.

All that is left is what then might be considered an eternal unbounded space of pure awareness . . . without any separate subject, object or even thought.[25]

[21] "This omniscient Ātmā is neither born, nor does he die; he has not originated from anywhere or anything. He is unborn, eternal, everlasting and ancient; he is not destroyed even when the body is destroyed." **Katha Upanishad, 2.18, Bhaktivedanta Ashram, IndiaDivine.org**
"The soul is neither born, nor does it ever die; nor having once existed, does it ever cease to be. The soul is without birth, eternal, immortal, and ageless. It is not destroyed when the body is destroyed." **Bhagavad Gita 2.20, holy-bhagavad-gita.org**

[22] **A Course in Miracles** tells us we have never left heaven. **A Course in Miracles, Manual for Teachers**, Clarification of Terms, 5.1

[23] The person is merely the result of a misunderstanding.
In reality, there is no such thing.
Feelings, thoughts and actions race before the watcher in endless succession, leaving traces in the brain and creating an illusion of continuity.
A reflection of the watcher in the mind creates the sense of 'I' and the person acquires an apparently independent existence.
In reality there is no person, only the watcher identifying himself with the 'I' and the 'mine'.
The teacher tells the watcher: you are not this, there is nothing of yours in this, except the little point of 'I am', which is the bridge between the watcher and his dream. 'I am this, I am that' is dream, while pure 'I am' has the stamp of reality on it.
You have tasted so many things -- all came to naught. Only the sense 'I am' persisted -- unchanged. Stay with the changeless among the changeful, until you are able to go beyond.
Break the bonds of memory and self-identification and the shell will break by itself.
There is a centre that imparts reality to whatever it perceives.
All you need is to understand that you are the source of reality, that you give reality instead of getting it, that you need no support and no confirmation.
Things are as they are, because you accept them as they are.
Stop accepting them and they will dissolve.
- **Nisargadatta**, "I AM THAT"

[24] George **Gurdjieff** quoted by student P.D. Ouspensky. Gurdjieff also said: "You are in prison. If you wish to get out of prison, the first thing you must do is realize that you are in prison. If you think you are free, you can't escape." Gurdjieff also put this more strongly, 'You are the prison."

[25] *"I and my Father are one."* **New Testament, John 10:30 (KJV)**

How

Surrender beliefs and open to intuitive wisdom

A first step is releasing long-cherished beliefs and convictions held since infancy and childhood about who we identify ourselves as being and about 'the way it is'. This becomes easier when we realize that, as children, we accepted without questioning what we were told, even when it flew in the face of what we instinctively and intuitively knew and recognized about the already wholeness of our essential aware selves.

When we give up mental knowing and learned beliefs, we make space for our natural intuitive knowingness to be present.

Openness to, and readiness for, the right teacher, teachings and grace

Receiving the teachings and/or blessings/grace/transmission of a guide, or teacher, however briefly, who has already awakened can be an immense – and usually indispensable – aid. We are so accustomed to seeking with our minds, but what is sought now comes from before and beyond the mind.

Such grace will usually come from one who is already self-realized, but it can also come from another source or combination of sources, such as nature, life experiences, one's studies and/or even from inside oneself.

This also requires the use of discrimination, discernment, and resonance to understand and intuitively recognize the truth of such teachings and grace. Grace can come as well in forms the mind may have thought of as being negative and it can take the 'push' or 'pull' of such shocks to motivate us to new clarity and evolution.

The resultant awakening speaks of one being ripe and open enough to receive and benefit and of the resonance one has oneself with such grace, so this is really the recognition of the oneness of like with like.[26]

Meditation/Dhyana – becoming pure boundless 'space'

We can practice and experience the meditative/dhyana state through withdrawing attention from the mind's thoughts and external inputs received through perception. As our personalities and egos, with their desires, attachments, karma and vasanas[27], are all parts of the mind, then we are also withdrawing our identification from these.

When we close our eyes, stepping back also from the other senses and the mind, what we are left with is an alive space which is pure awareness alone. This requires following no practice, but simply shifting from outer attention and activity to that 'space' of inner still awareness which is a oneness without boundaries. That awareness at source is always with us. It is with us in our waking activities but forgotten in the distractions of the mind and pull of the senses. It is even with us in deep sleep, but unnoticed because it has no separate object to be aware of.

This experience of oneness is not dual with a separate experiencer and an experience – it is BEING oneness, pure with nothing else present to dilute it – limitless eternal awareness alive to itself.

This is becoming the 'space' – space as me, rather than body or mind as me; space is free, body and mind are not free – and it is simply 'space' not *my* 'space'.

Use attention to move progressively from mind to feeling to awareness

An important part of the journey 'home' comes through shifting the focus of our attention from being almost exclusively in our minds (thinking) and senses (perceptions of what is outside of us) into our feeling selves – the alive and energetic being we are which is independent of the mind. The mind is caught in a conceptual realm, while our feeling self has a **here and now** alive presence.

A simple way to come back to your feeling self is to direct your attention so it becomes aware of any part of your body, such as a toe, a forearm, the stomach or heart, or the back of your head. When you do this, you will find you can instantly be present in any point of your body and feel its energetic aliveness, the temperature and any pressure felt at that point and often even a sense of the blood pulsing through it.

You can then progressively move this instant awareness of any single part of your body to any other part, such as from your foot to your leg, then to your chest and on to your arm or to your forehead.

Now, instead of focusing this attention on any single part of the body, have it be present in any whole section of your body, such as all of one leg and foot, or the whole of your torso, or an entire arm and hand, or your neck and head together. You will find it easy to spread your attention so as to have an awareness of the whole of these major parts of your body.

Next, expand further by spreading this attentive awareness so it permeates through the whole of your body, from head to shoulders to fingertips, then down your torso and legs to your toes. Suddenly, you find you can be present throughout all of your feeling self. When living so much in our minds, we forget our feeling selves but, in spreading our attention this way, we find the treasure of a whole realm of vibrant awareness.

Establishing our awareness in our feeling presence has taken us away from our mind and external perceptions of the senses. We can bask in this feeling self of ours in a relaxed posture, sitting or lying down, with closed eyes for at least a few minutes or even longer. When doing this we are not actively controlling or trying to stop thoughts, but we find that by maintaining our attention on our feeling presence throughout the body, thoughts either spontaneously stop arising or they might just arise and then disappear without our really noticing or grasping any of them, as we would normally do when keeping our attention in the mind.

At this point, still as relaxed as possible and with closed eyes, we can make the last move with our attention, shifting from our feeling presence to that which has been aware of it, the source of our awareness, our subjective essence. Some call this returning 'home' to being the knower or the experiencer. Others call it awareness of awareness.

Be present when transiting from sleep to waking

Another means of reconnecting to this state is to maintain alertness when transiting from sleep to waking.[28]

We are in the state of pure awareness in deep sleep, but not conscious of it. When we awaken, there is an extremely brief transition from sleep to the mind and personality re-engaging, when we remember and re-establish who we are in our waking state. When we 'catch' that brief instant, which is awareness before the mind starts, it becomes a benchmark for us and, with practice, the duration of this state of just awareness can be extended for longer and longer periods.

Find and identify with the unchanging

Find that which is unchanging. The sleeping state changes to the dreaming state and then those two states change to the waking state. You are present in each of the states – 'I am sleeping', 'I am dreaming', and 'I am awake'. What is always present and unchanging throughout every state is YOU.

Shift identification from what is external back to your essential self. This means voluntarily making the choice to stop being drawn outward by thoughts and perceptions which take us away from 'home' to hopes and fears in the world and instead turn back inwards to your subjective aware essence.

Realize that unchanging as your true identity and the changing mind and body as the false ones. What is changing will have an ending. What is unchanging is eternal.

[26] Gurdjieff said you need someone who is already in a higher state to help you out of the prison we do not even realize we are in, which he also likened to a state of hypnotized sleep.
A Course in Miracles speaks of 'The Holy Spirit' being a link between God and man in bringing light to the world and communicating truth. It says Jesus is the Holy Spirit's manifestation and it abides in the part of our minds representing our Self. **A Course in Miracles, Manual for Teachers**, Clarification of Terms, 6.1 and 4.

[27] Vasanas are literally the wishes or desires we have. In Advaita they also refer to the sub-conscious or unconscious tendencies, the impulses and drivers, we bring into this life at birth, before even becoming rational or acquiring a personality.

[28] In sleep there was no world, no ego (no limited self), and no trouble. Something wakes up from that happy state and says 'I'. To that ego the world appears. Being a speck in the world a man wants more and gets into trouble.
How happy he was before the rising of the ego! Only the rise of the ego is the cause of the present trouble. Let him trace the ego to its source and he will reach that undifferentiated happy state which is sleepless sleep.
The Self remains ever the same, here and now. There is nothing more to be gained. Because the limitations have wrongly been assumed there is the need to transcend them. - **Sri Ramana Maharshi**, Talk 63.

Who we are at source is not a goal to be attained

It is who we already are. We must just realize or remember it, largely by de-identifying with what we are not (our mistaken identification).

We will still have a mind and a body in what can be called relative reality, but they are tools to enjoy and use while we have them – they are no longer our primary identity and they no longer run us.

Awakening to our reality as just this pure awareness does not deny we may also be associated with a temporary relative physical and mental self . . . which is a precious vehicle giving us the potential of coming back to our REAL identity.[29]

Who I really am has never been born . . . and consequently can never die.[30]

I am constant present reality as pure awareness – formless, nameless and eternal.

This reality is characterized by the great peace experienced during deep dreamless sleep when awareness of the body and mind are absent . . . but a pure awareness of 'nothingness' remains present.[31]

---

[29] **A Course in Miracles** speaks of the purpose of time being precisely this attainment.

[30] *"There is no death of anyone, but only in appearance, even as there is no birth of any, save only in seeming. **The change from being to becoming seems to be birth, and the change from becoming to being seems to be death, but in reality no one is ever born, nor does one ever die.***"*
- words attributed to **Apollonius of Tyana** (1st century CE):
http://gnosis.org/library/grs-mead/apollonius/apollonius_mead_16.htm

[31] *"What is the state beyond bliss?*
It is the state of unceasing peace of mind which is found in the state of absolute quiescence, jagrat-sushupti (lit. sleep with awareness) which resembles inactive deep sleep.
In this state, in spite of the activity of the body and the senses, there is no external awareness, like a child immersed in sleep (who is not conscious of the food given to him by his mother).
A yogi who is in this state is inactive even while engaged in activity.
This is also called sahaja nirvikalpa samadhi (natural state of absorption in oneself without concepts)."
- Spiritual Instruction from **Ramana Maharshi**.

Being 'space'

The closest description in a dimensional sense is a oneness which is a single 'substance' or, more simply, pure 'space'.[32]

'Being is awareness. It cannot be experienced as an object, as a sensation, or mental state because it is non-dual. We can only BE it. It is always available if we drop all thinking, wanting or any form of mental activity for a moment and rest as IT.'

- Ramana Maharshi

Priest: What does Ma consider the most essential thing in life?

MA: To try and find out 'Who am I'.

To try to know that which has brought into existence one's body and mind.

This also may become the search after God.

But the first thing is to conceive the desire to know oneself.

Finding one's Self, one has found God and finding God one has found one's Self - the one Atma.

Q: Are there many people who succeed in this quest?

MA: Quite a number attain to some siddhi [a degree of attainment] or mukti [liberation], but only one in ten million arrives at complete Realization.

It is very, very rare.

Question: Do you think you have reached the ultimate state?

MA: (Laughs)

Whatever you believe me to be, that I am.

Q: From what moment did you have that Realization?

MA: When was I not?

- Anandamayi Ma

---

[32] *"19. Without parts, without activity, peaceful, without sound, without impurities, the supreme bridge to immortality, like a fire that burns without fuel, is He.*

20. When man rolls up space as if it were a piece of leather, only then perhaps he can put an end to his sorrows, other than by not knowing Brahman." **Svetasvatara Upanishad, Chapter 6, Hinduwebsite.com**

Part 3

Being Our Essential Self

"You are the sole witness to all that is, and all that comes to pass.

You are forever free.

Your only bondage is not seeing this."

~ The Ashtavakra Gita

Illustrating the Relationship between Reality and the Material World

In 1886 Ernst Mach did a sketch of 'View from the left eye' which became better known after being reproduced in Karl Pearson's 1892 *Grammar of Science*.

Fig. 8.

In Mach's sketch we can see him looking down at his body and the rest of the room surrounding that with his sketching pencil in his right hand. What is unusual about this sketch is that bordering the top, right side and part of the bottom is just what he could see from his left eye of his eyebrow, the side of his nose and part of his moustache. With his astonishingly simple sketch, Mach is drawing our attention back to the reality of the one who is seeing, and who not only cannot see himself, but is looking out from an aware but empty space.

Douglas Harding explored and clarified the meaning of Mach's revelatory sketch in his Headless Way teachings.

Reality as awareness witness of the Maya/Illusion of manifested creation (adapted from a diagram from headless.org)

He pointed out that we only see our head when we see a reflection of it, as in a mirror. It is our awareness which sees the reflection of ourself in the mirror. We are aware of our face and head because we see it in the mirror.

However, we also see reflected in the mirror what is around the reflected head.

Why do we not also own those surrounding parts just as we do the reflected head?

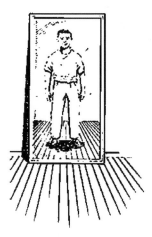

From 'The Mirror', Headless Way, headless.org

And if we own everything reflected in the mirror as part of ourselves as our awareness, then it follows we must also own what our awareness sees in front of us, as the mirror, the room and the whole of the world that is in our experience.[33]

Douglas restated his adaptation of Ernst Mach's sketch with one which showed the two extremes, paradoxically both versions of Oneness: I Am All and I Am Not.

I am all is the oneness we are in manifested reality.

I am not is the oneness we are in space, sometimes referred to as the void or emptiness.

What is common to both extremes is 'I'. Our 'I' contains everything in our waking reality and our 'I' is all there is in our inner centre or core.

This 'I' is formless, nameless and eternal – unchanging. The pure awareness that is 'I' looking out at these words now is the same awareness that was present when we first saw the world as newborn infants. Moreover, it is the same awareness present when there are no senses or mind to discern objects or thoughts, such as during deep sleep and was the same awareness that was there even before we were born.

What this means is that the who we may have thought we were throughout our whole life as time-bound human beings, together with manifested creation around us, has simply been passing through who we are as eternal unchanging reality. This would similarly be true for any and all incarnations experienced.

Moreover, it suggests we not only come into this world with our physical bodies as something of a spacesuit our soul puts on, but that all of 'our' changing worlds we perceive about us are just our own reflections on the mirror surface of our awareness. Similarly, each 'separate' person will have their own different perceived reality reflected back to their individual awareness according to their beliefs, culture, nationality, etc.

I Am All AND I Am Not, from Headless Way, headless.org

---

[33] Without question, the one "thing" to which we give the greatest value, out of all proportion, is the "thing" we see when we look in the mirror. The body in the mirror is not our Identity, any more than Macbeth is the identity of the actor playing that role. The one and only Identity is That which is being the consciousness that perceives the body in the mirror. Awareness is the action-activity of That which is being the body in the mirror, the mirror itself, the door frame, the house, the world and the entire universe, every bit included in (as) the Awareness that looks in the mirror. Identity, then, is infinitely more than a single outline in the consciousness of images and things. As a matter of fact, Identity has no more to do with a particular body-outline than the picture hanging on the wall. The Identity-being-I is being every object of perception. It is well, we say again, that the images in the mirror (and all other objects of perception) are neither real nor unreal; they are nothing in themselves. The "value," the "something," is That which is being images! The "That" is Reality, Supernal Isness, God. *From A Guide to Awareness & Tranquillity, by* William Samuel

Understanding the Levels

Spiritual teachings are expressed from the inner self, that pure awareness, which is before and senior to the normal mind. They are addressed to that same inner self which all individuals possess as their common birthright but are usually either not aware of or pay no attention to.

The three basic levels
The teachings speak of people having three basic realms or levels:

An inner essential core or Self of pure awareness. It is also referred to as spirit consciousness, spiritual heart and home and is the source of intuition and inspiration.[34] In the **Bhagavad Gita**, it is represented by Krishna. Once awake to itself, this inner self is self-aware (conscious awareness), but is without physical dimensions, form or colors. It is timeless, unchanging and a state of oneness. Its awareness of itself is not divided into subject, verb and object, but is one.

A physical level in manifested creation, which includes the world, the solar system, the universe, everything made up of atoms and molecules, the body, the senses, perceptions of and stimuli from the external and physical sensations of the body itself. The one who is aware of the physical through the stimuli and senses is the changeless inner self, which is outside of and before the mind.

The mental/emotional level, which is not one's own, but acquired externally from one's family, education, society culture and other surroundings. This makes up one's personality and ego, likes and dislikes, and includes using the mind for day-to-day physical survival and activities requiring intellect. This can be thought of as 'surface-mind consciousness', which is not aware of the deeper spiritual heart or spirit consciousness but will be aware of spiritual inquiry on the mind level. It lives in separation, believing itself to be a body, and so is fear-based. In the ***Bhagavad Gita***, it is represented by Arjuna.

The mental/emotional level is the one least referred to in teachings, unless they are directed to helping deal with psychological issues like understanding success and failure, how to live our outer life in a more wholistic way and living in accordance with spiritual principles. ("*. . . the mind is the seat of logic and rationality, a gateway into the world of illusions and emotions.*" – Srinivas Arka).

However, the intellect part of the mind – the part that has the power of discrimination – is closest to our essential self in nature and when used in its purest sense can be the vehicle which can take us home.

As the reality is that there is only the self, pure being, sometimes called the absolute I am. Everything else emanates from that. It can be referred to as consciousness, life, love, awareness. It is unchanging and formless oneness, where there is no space or time.

The fetus in the womb, and even when a newborn baby, continues to be self-aware consciousness not recognizing any form or name labels, neither for itself, nor for any other or anything else separate whatsoever. It is literally still experiencing a oneness which includes its own mother.[35]

The opening of the physical senses, especially its eyes, together with a developing relationship with its mother is the start of the development of the baby's mind, which separates into me and you, this and that, here and there. It goes on to develop preferences, likes and dislikes, and an identification with being the mind as a separate form with its own name label grows. Soon, certainly by its second year, most infants have almost completely forgotten the oneness they started from – and which is still there but hidden by the mind. Here, the ego takes over.

The mind is born out of the self and is like the senses, but senior to them and the receiver of them. The mind points outward and so listens only to perceptions, thoughts and emotions.

The mind is made up of habits, which are impulses coming from the self. These impulses of the mind are thoughts, or *vrittis*[36] and *vasanas*, the seeds of which create and grow into forms in the realm of time and space. They make up the form of the body and all the other forms of the world and universe. All these forms, being in time and space, are subject to birth and dissolution.

The mind is never really separate from the self, but it can believe it to be so and take over from the self, identifying with the body it created and thinking it is separate.

When we identify with being a mind and body, we create a prison for ourselves in time and space. The mind creates its world through imagination. All fears and suffering are linked to time and space. We have forgotten our divine self, the space of intelligence and love, the pure I am of our being which is eternal, was never born and will never die.

When the mind, which associates itself with the body, tries to control, we identify with fears – especially that of death.

For this reason, our highest purpose is to remember the self and to establish ourselves in that self, where there is happiness and peace. When our mind is open and the self is the base of our identity, the mind can be used – and the senses enjoyed – without our losing ourselves in being a temporal mind and body.

Accordingly, we should avoid negative thoughts and cherish positive ones, avoid judging and harming others and cherish respect for all life. Spiritual evolution is the gradual purification of the mind's attachments and misconceptions, often referred to as *vasanas*.

Once established in the self, we then let the mind do its job through the senses. The senses' purpose is to look after the body, not to become lost in seeking power or possessions to protect itself from its fears.

---

[34] " . . .the kingdom of God is within you." **New Testament, Luke 17:21 (KJV)**

[35] "*Jesus said: The old man will not hesitate to ask a seven-day-old baby about the place of life and he will live.*" **Gospel of Thomas, Saying 4a, translation by Stevan Davies.**

[36] Vrittis are waves or, literally, 'whirlpools', of thoughts surfacing and disturbing the calm of mental awareness.

Ways of being

Living from the mind

. . . blocks and assumes the role of our inner self

I am	Mind	All externals
Inner Self	Personality	Body – World
Our divine spark	Illusion	Seen as separate
Krishna	Ignorance	via the mind.
Atma	Beliefs	Thought,
Timeless,	Arjuna	desires,
changeless,	Blocks one's	fears
formless	Inner Self	control us
awareness		

When we are based in the mind, we see and interpret our body, the world and universe from it based on our concepts and beliefs, likes and dislikes, desires and fears. Our essential core (self/sun) is hidden, blocked by the cloud of our mind's ignorance and beliefs.

Living from the inner self

– externals experienced in and as part of awareness, while mind is our subservient tool

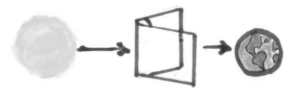

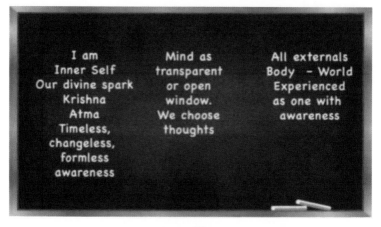

I am	Mind as	All externals
Inner Self	transparent	Body – World
Our divine spark	or open	Experienced
Krishna	window.	as one with
Atma	We choose	awareness
Timeless,	thoughts	
changeless,		
formless		
awareness		

Living as the eternal self

However, realizing one is the unborn outside of time and space, one's beingness is known to and by itself as the unified oneness, like the space one experiences in closed-eye meditation.[37]

Full identification with being this self means one transcends the old illusory identity as a human being, realizing it never actually existed.[38] A corollary of this is that all one's thought attachments, karma and vasanas are also surrendered.

While there continues to be any association with a physical body and manifested creation when eyes are open in the wakened state, one acts responsibly in worldly terms without identifying with being the physical, realizing everything within one's experience, however illusory, is oneself.

This can be likened to being a conscious dreamer, aware that all the forms in the dream are one's own projections, but always conscious that the only reality is the source of those projections, the eternal – unborn and undying – self-aware Knower.[39]

[37] The title of a book of talks by Nisargadatta reflects this state: *The Experience of Nothingness*.

[38] A Course in Miracles tells us it is the body which gives rise to the idea of separation and that spirit, as being of God, is eternal and unborn. **A Course in Miracles**, Manual for Teachers, Clarification of Terms 1.1-3.

[39] The title of one of the earliest books with talks of Ramana Maharshi, *Conscious Immortality*, describes the state.

Part 4

Excerpts from teachers and traditions

The answer to "Who am I?" will reveal one's true nature. One who has the desire for his well-being, to be liberated from mental bondage, acquires the knowledge of the Self, sooner or later, and avoids birth and death. Man alone has the ability to think and to understand his true nature. To attain Self-realisation is to fulfil one's duty, which is to live as Reality while in a human form. The One who resides in each heart is Reality and He alone is real. He who takes refuge in the seen perishes, and he who takes refuge in Reality attains eternal peace.

- Siddharameshwar Maharaj

"There are two selves, the apparent self and the real Self. Of these it is the real Self, and he alone, who must be felt as truly existing. To the man who has felt him as truly existing he reveals his innermost nature"

- Katha Upanishad 2:3:13

"Every living being longs always to be happy, untainted by sorrow; and everyone has the greatest love for himself, which is solely due to the fact that happiness is his real nature. Hence, in order to realize that inherent and untainted happiness, which indeed he daily experiences when the mind is subdued in deep sleep, it is essential that he should know himself. For obtaining such knowledge the inquiry 'Who am I?' in quest of the Self is the best means."

- Sri Ramana Maharshi

Awareness

To be a living being is not the ultimate state: there is something beyond, much more wonderful, which is neither being nor non-being, neither living nor not-living. It is a state of pure awareness, beyond the limitations of space and time. Once the illusion that the body-mind is oneself is abandoned, death loses its terror; it becomes a part of living. **Nisargadatta**

If our mind dwells in limpid awareness, with no thought of past or future, without being attracted by external objects or occupied by mental constructions, it will dwell in primordial simplicity. In this state, there is no need for the iron hand of forced vigilance to immobilize our thoughts. "Buddhahood," it is said, "is the natural simplicity of the mind." **Dilgo Khyentse Rinpoche**

Prayer is an awareness of that which IS by seeing it – not making it so. **Joel Goldsmith**

Thoughts are not necessarily a distraction. Thoughts are arising in this present awareness and dissolving back into it. The silence remains untouched, unstained, immaculate. Thoughts are only a problem if you are preoccupied with them, giving them all your attention, believing in the entity of 'me' around which the thoughts swirl. **Catherine Ingram**

. . . the man who realizes self-awareness feels that he is no more the obedient servant of blind impulse but is his own master. **Chang Chen-chi**

A True Master does not tell you to do this or that. Already, you are bewildered going to motivational speakers, satsang teachers, and visiting one guru after another. The Master simply brings attention to your nature as Being-Awareness and invites you to rest in your own Heart. **Ramana Maharshi**

The Atman is that by which the universe is pervaded, but which nothing pervades, which causes all things to shine, but which all things cannot make to shine. **Shankara**

By what means do this body and mind perceive? Can they perceive with the eyes, ears . . . ? No. Your own Nature, being essentially pure and utterly still, is capable of this perception. **Hui-hai**

You each have a pair of ears, but what have you ever heard with them? You each have a tongue, but what have you ever said with it? . . . From whence, then, do all these forms, voices, odors and tastes come? **Fo-yen**

Only God has seeing, hearing. **Al-Arabi**

Being

Be still and know that I am God. **Old Testament, Psalm 46**

Ramana Maharshi

- Your duty is to be and not to be this or that. 'I am that I am' sums up the whole truth. The method is summed up in the words 'Be still'. What does stillness mean? It means destroy yourself. Because any form or shape is the cause for trouble. Give up the notion that 'I am so and so'. All that is required to realize the Self is to be still. What can be easier than that?

- There is no greater mystery than this: Being Reality ourselves, we seek to gain Reality.

- It is not a matter of becoming but of Being.

He walks without feet, He sees without eyes, He hears without ears, and eats without a mouth. **Anandamayi Ma**

The eye by which I see God is the same as the eye by which God sees me. My eye and God's eye are one and the same - one in seeing, one in knowing, one in loving. **Meister Eckhart**

God is neither soul nor angel ... nor can He be described or understood ... He neither stands still nor moves ... He is none of the things that have no being, none of the things that have being... Nor is there any way by which we can reach Him through reason or understanding... **The Cloud of Unknowing**

The ten thousand things are born of being.

Being is born of not being. **Lao-tzu**

Knowing

When the Self is seen, heard, thought of, known, everything is known. **Brihadaranyaka Upanishad**

He who knows everything except himself, lacks everything. **Gospel of Thomas**

He who knows himself sees his whole existence to be His existence and does not see any change take place in his own essence or attributes, seeing that he was not the existence of his essence, but was merely ignorant of the knowledge of himself. For when you 'know yourself', your egoism is taken away and you know that you are not other than God. For, if you had had an independent existence, so that you did not require to cease to be or to 'know yourself', then you would be a Lord. God forbid that He should have created a Lord beside Himself. **Ibn 'Arabi**

Looking (within)

Neither shall they say, Lo here! or, Lo there! for, behold, the Kingdom of God is within you. **Jesus New Testament**

If those who lead you say, 'See, the Kingdom is in the sky,' then the birds of the sky will precede you. If they say to you, 'It is in the sea,' then the fish will precede you. Rather, the Kingdom is inside of you, and it is outside of you. When you come to know yourselves, then you will become known, and you will realize that it is you who are the sons of the living Father. But if you will not know yourselves, you dwell in poverty and it is you who are that poverty.' *Jesus, Gospel of Thomas, 3*

If you cannot find the truth where you are,
Where do you expect to find it?
Truth is not far away; it is ever present.
It is not something to be attained
Since not one of your steps leads away from it.

Dogen

I gazed into my own heart; there I saw Him; He was nowhere else.
Rumi

Ramana Maharshi

- The only useful purpose of the present birth is to turn within and realize the Self.

- The answer to your problem is to see who has it.

- Forgetfulness of the Self is the source of all misery.

How may we perceive our own nature? That which perceives is your own nature. **Hui-hai**

The sage all the time sees and hears no more than an infant sees and hears. **Lao-tzu**

Observe things as they are and don't pay attention to other people. **Huang-po**

What I call perfection of vision is not seeing other but oneself. **Chuang-tzu**

Whatever appears to you in the universe is due solely to that great Light within you. **Anandamayi Ma**

When we look outside of that on which we depend we ignore our unity; looking outward we see many faces; look inward and all is one head. If a man could but be turned about, he would see at once God and himself and the All. **Plotinus**

God made the senses turn outwards, man therefore looks outwards, not into himself. But occasionally a daring soul, desiring immortality, has looked back and found himself. He is the imperishable among things that perish. Life of all life, He, though one, satisfies every man's desire. He that dare discover Him within, knows peace; what other dare know peace?" **Katha Upanishad**

My Guru ordered me to attend to the sense 'I am' and to give attention to nothing else. I just obeyed. I did not follow any particular course of breathing, or meditation, or study of scriptures. Whatever happened, I would turn away my attention from it and remain with the sense 'I am'. It may look too simple, even crude. My only reason for doing it was that my Guru told me so. Yet it worked. **Nisargadatta**

You examine the face of heaven and earth but you don't know what is where you are, and you ignore the present moment. **Gospel of Thomas**

Thou art as a mirage in the desert that the thirsty man taketh to be water until he cometh unto it and findeth it to be nothing, and where he thought it to be, there findeth he God. Even so, if thou wert to examine thyself, thou wouldst find it to be naught, and there wouldst thou find God. **Al-Alawi**

People seek it far away – what a pity!

They are like him who, in the midst of water,

Cries out in thirst so imploringly. **Hakuin**

See, where thou nothing seest;

Go, where thou canst not go;

Hear, where there is no sound;

Then where God speaks art thou.

Angelus Silesius

Question: Was Christ a Jnani or a yogi? Can a Jnani heal people like he did?

Robert Adams: Never mind Christ.

Who are you?

Where did you come from?

What are you all about?

Leave Christ alone.

Leave the healing alone.

Understand who you are.

Try to find yourself then you'll understand Christ.

By understanding Christ but not understanding your Self will be folly.

You'll never have the right answer.

But by understanding your Self you will understand what Christ is all about.

It always goes back to you.

You are the one.

Work within yourself.

Ask yourself,

"To whom do all these thoughts come? Where do all these mind boggling thoughts come, these opinions, these questions?

To whom do they come?

Who is thinking them?

What is their source?"

Go back within yourself.

Inquire within yourself.

Find out for your Self.

It makes no difference what I say. It's all up to you.

You are the one.

Dive deep within yourself and everything will be revealed to you.

Robert Adams

Love

According to Buddhism, ultimate and unconditioned love can only be achieved through a realization of Voidness (sunyata). Because there are no sentient beings to be pitied, Buddha has the greatest pity; because from the very beginning no sentient beings ever existed, Buddha 'came down' to earth to save sentient beings.
Chang Chen-chi

Nisargadatta

- I find that somehow, by shifting the focus of attention, I become the very thing I look at, and experience the kind of consciousness it has; I become the inner witness of the thing. I call this capacity of entering other focal points of consciousness, love; you may give it any name you like. Love says "I am everything". Wisdom says "I am nothing". Between the two, my life flows. Since at any point of time and space I can be both the subject and the object of experience, I express it by saying that I am both, and neither, and beyond both.

- When you know beyond all doubting that the same life flows through all that is and you are that life, you will love all naturally and spontaneously. When you realize the depth and fullness of your love of yourself, you know that every living being and the entire universe are included in your affection.

- 'I am' itself is God. The seeking itself is God. In seeking you discover that you are neither body nor mind, but the love of the self in you for the self in all. The two are one. The consciousness in you and the consciousness in me, apparently two, really one, seek unity and that is love.

Meditation/Prayer

The mind of one meditating on a single object becomes one-pointed. And one-pointedness of mind leads to abidance in the self. **Ramana Maharshi**

Questioner: All teachers advise to meditate. What is the purpose of meditation?

Maharaj: We know the outer world of sensations and actions, but of our inner world of thoughts and feelings we know very little. The primary purpose of meditation is to become conscious of, and familiar with, our inner life. The ultimate purpose is to reach the source of life and consciousness.

Incidentally, practice of meditation affects deeply our character. We are slaves to what we do not know; of what we know we are masters. Whatever vice or weakness in ourselves we discover and understand its causes and its workings, we overcome it by the very knowing; the unconscious dissolves when brought into the conscious. The dissolution of the unconscious releases energy; the mind feels adequate and become quiet.

Q: What is the use of a quiet mind?

M: When the mind is quiet, we come to know ourselves as the pure witness. We withdraw from the experience and its experiencer and stand apart in pure awareness, which is between and beyond the two. The personality, based on self-identification, on imagining oneself to be something: 'I am this, I am that', continues, but only as a part of the objective world. Its identification with the witness snaps.

... Meditation is a sattvic activity and aims at complete elimination of tamas (inertia) and rajas (motivity). Pure sattva (harmony) is perfect freedom from sloth and restlessness.

- **Nisargadatta**, chapter 6, I AM THAT

" . . . when you pray, go into your room, close the door and pray to your Father, who is unseen." *Jesus, Matthew 6:6, New Testament*

Mind/No mind

Ramana Maharshi

- The life of man is what it is. That which is, is. All the trouble arises by having a conception of it. Mind comes in. It has a conception. All trouble follows. If you are as you are, without a mind and its conceptions about various things, all will be well with you. If you seek the source of the mind, then all questions will be solved.

- It is the nature of the mind to wander. You are not the mind. The mind springs up and sinks down. It is impermanent, transitory, whereas you are eternal. To inhere in the Self is the thing. Never mind the mind, In the realized man the mind may be active or inactive, the Self alone remains for him.

Buddhahood is attained when there is no mind to be used for the task. **Hui-chung**

How can there be merits and demerits for me who am without organs, without mind, changeless and formless? **Shankara**

When you keep a clear mind, the whole universe is you, you are the universe. So you have already attained enlightenment. Wanting enlightenment is only thinking it is something extra. The truth is right before your eyes. **Zen Master Seung Sahn**

Mind is only a cloud that hides the sun of Truth. Man is, in fact, God playing the fool. When he chooses, he liberates himself. **Ram Dass**

If there were no eye, what? If there were no ear, what? If there were no mouth, what? If there were no mind, what? If one has to face such circumstances and knows how to act, then one is in the company of the ancient Patriarchs and Buddhas. Anyone in that company is satisfied. **Blue Cliff Records**

Only have no mind of any kind, and this is known as undefiled knowledge. **Huang-po**

Which of you by mental effort can add a span to his height? -**Jesus**, **Matthew 6:25-29,** *The Original New Testament***, Schonfield)**

Mirror/Reflection

Rumi

- Let go care and become wholly clear of heart, like the face of a mirror without image and picture. When it has become clear of images, all images are contained in it; that clear-faced one is not ashamed of any man's face.

- The whole body will become like a mirror: it will become all eye and spiritual substance.

- After all, how long does a reflection remain in view? Make a practice of contemplating the origin of the reflection. This cheek and mole go back to the source thereof.

One can know oneself only with one's own eye of knowledge, and not with somebody else's. Does he who is Rama require the help of a mirror to know that he is Rama? **Ramana Maharshi**

Name and Form

Caste, creed, family and lineage do not exist in Brahman. Brahman has neither name nor form, transcends merit and demerit, is beyond time, space and the objects of sense-experience. Such is Brahman, and "thou art That". **Shankara**

The Tao that can be spoken is not the eternal Tao
The name that can be named is not the eternal name
The nameless is the origin of Heaven and Earth
The named is the mother of myriad things

Lao-tzu

When the kingdom of Pure Consciousness has been attained, form is revealed as the Essence itself. What was sorrow from the worldly point of view is now Viraha, separation from THAT; in other words, the agony of existing in a particular form. **Anandamayi Ma**

If you have the idea that you are something with form, that you are limited by this body, and that being within this body you have to see through these eyes, God and the world also will appear to you as form. If you realise you are without form, that you are unlimited, that you alone exist, that you are the eye, the infinite eye, what is there to be seen apart from the infinite eye? Apart from the eye there is nothing to be seen. **Ramana Maharshi** (Day by Day with Bhagavan. 18 April, 1946.)

No soul can have rest until it finds created things are empty. **Julian of Norwich**

Rumi

- His form has passed away, he has become a mirror: naught is there but the image of another's face.

- That head of clay is from the earth, and this pure Head from Heaven.

Is it not important to you to know whether you are a mere body or something else? Or maybe nothing at all? Don't you see that all your problems – food, clothing, shelter, family, friends, name, fame, security, survival – all these lose their meaning the moment you realize you may not be a mere body. **Nisargadatta**

Become pure till you neither are nor have this or that; then you are omnipresent and, being neither this nor that, are all things. **Eckhart**

All that has form, sound, color, may be classed under the head 'thing' ... But a man can attain to formlessness and vanquish death. And with that which is in possession of the eternal, how can mere things compare? **Chuang-tzu**

As rivers lose name and shape in the sea, wise men lose name a shape in God, glittering beyond all distance. **Mundaka Upanishad**

Oneness

Behold but One in all things; it is the second that leads you astray. **Kabir**

The fundamental delusion of humanity is to suppose that I am here and you are out there. **Yasutani Roshi**

When the Ten Thousand things are viewed in their oneness, we return to the Origin and remain where we have always been.   **Sen t'san**

He is not far from every one of us: for in him we live, and move, and have our being. **New Testament, Acts**

'I am God' is an expression of great humility. The man who says 'I am the slave of God' affirms two existences, his own and God's, but he that says 'I am God' has made himself non-existent and has given himself up and says 'I am naught, He is all: there is no being but God's.' This is extreme humility and self-abasement. **Rumi**

There is no chaos in the world except the chaos which your mind creates. It is self-created in the sense that at its very centre is the false idea of oneself as a thing different and separate from other things. In reality you are not a thing nor separate from other things. You are the infinite potentiality, the inexhaustible possibility. Because you are, all can be. The universe is but a partial manifestation of your limitless capacity to become.

Nisargadatta

Just as a human body has different parts such as the head, the hands, thighs, feet, fingers and toes, I find all of you representing my various limbs. **Anandamayi Ma**

Look, it cannot be seen – it is beyond form.

Listen, it cannot be heard – it is beyond sound.

Grasp, it cannot be held – it is intangible.

These three are indefinable.

Therefore, they are joined in one.

Lao-tzu

I and the Father are one. **Jesus, John 10:30, *The Original New Testament*, Schonfield**

Realization

That Self who is free from impurities, from old age and death, from grief and thirst and hunger, whose desire is true and whose desires come true -- that Self is to be sought after and enquired about, that Self is to be realized. **Chandogya Upanishad**

God is the substance of all form, God is infinite, God is all-inclusive, so the only thing to pray for is the realization of God. **Joel Goldsmith**

When you have caught the Supreme Moment, you suddenly come to know Who you really are. At that instant, when you have found your Self, the whole universe will have become yours. **Anandamayi Ma**

The whole great Earth is nothing but you. **Hsueh-feng**

You never enjoy the world aright till the sea itself floweth in your veins, till you are clothed with the heavens and crowned with the stars; and perceive yourself to be the sole heir of the whole world. **Thomas Traherne**

Ramana Maharshi

- Realization is getting rid of the delusion that you haven't realized.

- The state we call Realization is simply being one's self, not knowing anything or becoming anything.

- To know the truth of one's Self as the sole Reality, and to merge and become one with it, is the only true Realization.

- There is no mind to control if you realize the self. The mind having vanished, the self shines forth. In the realized man, the mind may be active or inactive, the self remains for him.

- If we talk of knowing the Self, there must be two Selves, one a knowing Self, another the Self which is known, and the process of knowing. The state we call realization is simply being oneself, not knowing anything or becoming anything. If one is realized, he is that which alone is and which alone always has been.

- Realization is to get rid of the delusion that you have not realized. Realization is to get rid of the delusion that you have not realized.

- Realization is our true nature. It is nothing new to be gained. What is new cannot be eternal. Therefore, there is no need to be doubting whether we would gain or lose the self.

- All know that the drop merges into the ocean, but few know that the ocean merges into the drop.

He that beholds his own Face – his light is greater than the light of the creatures.

Though he die his sight is everlasting, because his sight is the sight of the Creator. **Rumi**

Surrender

Surrender to your own Self, of which everything is an expression. **Nisargadatta**

See that I am God. See that I am in everything. See that I do everything. See that I have never stopped ordering my works, nor ever shall, eternally. See that I lead everything to the conclusion I ordained for it before time began, by the same power, wisdom and love with which I made it. How can anything be amiss? **Julian of Norwich**

Time and Space

Meister Eckhart

- The Now-moment in which God made the first man and the Now-moment in which the last man will disappear, and the Now-moment in which I am speaking are all one in God, in whom there is only one Now.

- Nothing so much hinders the soul's understanding of God as time and space. Time and space are parts of the whole but God is one. So if the soul is to recognize God, it must do so beyond space and time.

- Where time has never entered and no form was ever seen, at the centre, the summit of the soul, there God is creating the whole world.

Lay up for yourselves no store on earth, where locust-grub and moth destroy, and where thieves break in and steal. Rather lay up for yourselves store in heaven, where neither locust-grub nor moth destroys, and where no thieves break in and steal. For 'where your hoard is your heart is'. **Jesus, Matthew 6:20-24, *The Original New Testament*, Schonfield**

Three Anglo-Indian lady-doctors came from Bangalore. One of them had recently lost her husband in an air crash. She asked Sri Bhagavan:

Lady: Is there rebirth?

Bhagavan Sri Ramana: Do you know what birth is?

Lady: O yes, I know that I exist now, but I want to know if I'll exist in the future.

Bhagavan Sri Ramana: Past!.... Present!.... Future!....

Lady: Yes, today is the result of yesterday, the past, and tomorrow, the future, will be the result of today, the present. Am I right?

Bhagavan Sri Ramana: There is neither past nor future. There is only the Present. Yesterday was the present to you when you experienced it, and tomorrow will be also the present when you will experience it. Therefore experience takes place only in the present, and beyond presence, nothing exists.

Lady: Are then past and future mere imagination?

Bhagavan Sri Ramana: Yes, even the present is mere imagination, for the sense of time is purely mental. Space is similarly mental; therefore birth and rebirth, which take place in time and space cannot be other than imagination.

Ramana Maharshi, 3rd September, 1948

Unborn - Undying

The essence of your mind is not born so it will never die. It is not an existence, which is perishable. It is not an emptiness, which is a mere void. It has neither colour nor form. It enjoys no pleasures and suffers no pain. **Bassui**

In my birth all things were born and I was the cause of myself and of all things. **Meister Eckhart**

Owing to the I-am-the-body notion, death is feared as being the loss of Oneself. Birth and death pertain to the body only, but they are superimposed upon the Self. **Ramana Maharshi**

If you know yourself without existence or ceasing to be, then you know God. **Ibn 'Arabi**

He who sees the supreme Lord dwelling alike in all beings, and never perishing when they perish, he sees indeed. **Bhagavad Gita**

Gospel of Thomas

- I stood in the middle of the world and I appeared to them in the flesh. I found them all drunk. I found none that were thirsty. And my soul was troubled for the children of men, for they are blind in their hearts, and they do not see that they came empty into the world.

- You have abandoned the one who lives before you.

Monk: How does one get liberated?
Shih-t'ou: Who has ever put you in bondage?
Monk: What is the Pure Land?
Shih-t'ou: Who has ever defiled you?
Monk: What is Nirvana?
Shih-t'ou: Who has ever subjected you to birth and death?

Shih-t'ou

That Self who is free from impurities, from old age and death, from grief and thirst and hunger, whose desire is true and whose desires come true – that Self is to be sought after and inquired about, that self is to be realized. **Chandogya Upanishad**

We should be as very strangers to the thoughts, customs, and opinions of men in the world, as if we were but little children. So those things would appear to us only which do to children when they are first born. **Thomas Traherne**

Bankei

- The Buddha Mind, unborn and marvelously illuminating, is like a bright mirror. A mirror reflects whatever is in front of it. It is not deliberately trying to reflect things . . . Likewise, when the object being reflected is removed, the mirror is not trying <u>not</u> to reflect it – but when it is taken away, it does not appear in the mirror. The Unborn Buddha Mind is just like this.

- Disciple: How can I keep from regressing?
  Bankei: Abide in the Unborn Buddha Mind. When you do, you will not need to bother about advancing or regressing. In fact, when you abide in the Unborn, trying to advance is to regress instantly from the place of the Unborn.

- When you abide in the Unborn, you abide at the source of all Buddhas; so it is something wonderfully precious. There is no question of 'perishing' here, so when you abide in the Unborn, it is superfluous to speak about the Imperishable . . . What is not created cannot be destroyed.

- It is the Unborn which sees and hears, eats and sleeps.

If your bonds be not broken whilst living, what hope of deliverance in death?

It is but an empty dream that the soul shall have union with Him because it has passed from the body;

If He is found now, He is found then;

If not, we do but go to dwell in the City of Death. **Kabir**

Mr. M.: Theosophy speaks of 50 to 10,000-year intervals between death and rebirth. Why is this so?

Bhagavan: "There is no relation between the standard of measurements of one state of consciousness and another. All such measurements are hypothetical.

It is true that some individuals take more time and some less. But it must be distinctly understood that it is not the soul that comes and goes, but the thinking mind of the individual, which makes it appear to do so.

On whatever plane the mind happens to act, it creates a body for itself: in the physical world a physical body, in the dream world a dream body, which becomes wet with dream rain and sick with dream diseases.

After the death of the physical body, the mind remains inactive for some time, as in dreamless sleep, when it remains worldless and therefore bodiless. But soon it becomes active again in a new world and a new body – the astral, – till it assumes another body in what is called a "rebirth".

But the Jnani, the Self-Realized man, whose mind has already ceased to act, remains unaffected by death: it has dropped never to rise again to cause births and deaths. The chain of illusions has snapped forever for him."

It is now clear that there is neither real birth nor real death. It is the mind which creates and maintains the illusion of reality in this process until it is destroyed by Self-Realization.

- Ramana Maharshi, S.S. Cohen, Guru Ramana

Follow me and leave the dead to bury their dead. [response to a disciple who wanted leave to bury his father.] **Jesus, *Matthew ii:20 (The Original New Testament, Schonfield)***

Waking and Dreaming

Question: Is there no difference between waking and dream?

One should consider the universe to be like a dream. Except that waking is long and dreams are short, there is no difference [between the two states]. To the extent to which all the events which happen while one is awake appear to be real, to that same extent even the events that happen in dreams appear at that time to be real. In dreams, the mind assumes another body. In both the dream and the waking [states] thoughts and names-and-forms come into existence simultaneously.

Except that waking is dīrgha [long lasting] and dream is kṣaṇika [momentary or lasting for only a short while], there is no other difference [between these two mind-created states]. To the extent to which all the vyavahāras [doings, activities, affairs or occurrences] that happen in waking, seem [at this present moment] to be real, to that [same] extent even the vyavahāras that happen in dream seem at that time to be real. In dream, the mind takes another body [to be itself]. In both waking and dream thoughts and names-and-forms [the objects of the seemingly external world] occur in one time [that is, simultaneously]. **Ramana Maharshi (*Who Am I?* Michael James'** translation)

The fuller quote from Apollonius of Tyana
(part of which appeared as an endnote):

Among these letters is found one of some length addressed to Valerius, probably P. Valerius Asiaticus, consul in A.D. 70. It is a wise letter of philosophic consolation to enable Valerius to bear the loss of his son, and runs as follows:

"There is no death of anyone, but only in appearance, even as there is no birth of any, save only in seeming. **The change from being to becoming seems to be birth, and the change from becoming to being seems to be death, but in reality no one is ever born, nor does one ever die.** *It is simply a being visible and then invisible; the former through the density of matter, and the latter because of the subtlety of being - being which is ever the same, its only change being motion and rest. For being has this necessary peculiarity that its change is brought about by nothing external to itself; but whole becomes parts and parts become whole in the oneness of the all. And if it be asked: What is this which sometimes is seen and sometimes not seen, now in the same, now in the different?—it might be answered: It is the way of everything here in the world below that when it is filled out with matter it is visible, owing to the resistance of its density, but is invisible, owing to its subtlety, when it is rid of matter, though matter still surround it and flow through it in that immensity of space which hems it in but knows no birth or death.*

"But why has this false notion [of birth and death] remained so long without a refutation? Some think that what has happened through them, they have themselves brought about. They are ignorant that the individual is brought to birth through parents, not by parents, just as a thing produced through the earth is not produced from it. The change which comes to the individual is nothing that is caused by his visible surroundings, but rather a change in the one thing which is in every individual.

"And what other name can we give to it but primal being? 'Tis it alone that acts and suffers becoming all for all through all, eternal deity, deprived and wronged of its own self by names and forms. But this is a less serious thing than that a man should be bewailed, when he has passed from man to God by change of state and not by the destruction of his nature. The fact is that so far from mourning death you ought to honour it and reverence it. The best and the fittest way for you to honour death is now to leave the one who's gone to God, and set to work to play the ruler over those left in your charge as you were wont to do. It would be a disgrace for such a man as you to owe your cure to time and not to reason, for time makes even common people cease from grief. The greatest things is a strong rule, and of the greatest rulers he is best who first can rule himself. And how is it permissible to wish to change what has been brought to pass by will of God? If there's a law in things, and there is one, and it is God who has appointed it, the righteous man will have no wish to try to change good things, for such a wish is selfishness, and counter to the law, but he will think that all that comes to pass is a good thing. On! heal yourself, give justice to the wretched and console them; so shall you dry your tears. You should not set your private woes above your public cares, but rather set your public cares before your private woes. And see as well what consolation you already have! The nation sorrows with you for your son. Make some return to those who weep with you; and this you will more quickly do if you will cease from tears than if you still persist. Have you not friends? Why! you have yet another son. Have you not even still the one that's gone? You have! — will answer anyone who really thinks. For 'that which is' doth cease not – nay is just for the very fact that it will be for aye; or else the 'is not' is, and how could that be when the 'is' doth never cease to be?

"Again it will be said you fail in piety to God and are unjust. 'Tis true. You fail in piety to God, you fail in justice to your boy; nay more, you fail in piety to him as well. Would'st know what death is? Then make me dead and send me off to company with death, and if you will not change the dress you've put on it, [That is his idea of death.] you will have straightway made me better than yourself." [The text of the last sentence is very obscure].

- words attributed to Apollonius of Tyana (1st century CE):
http://gnosis.org/library/grs-mead/apollonius/apollonius_mead_16.htm

The above quote is from a section of the letters in *APOLLONIUS OF TYANA, The Philosopher Explorer and Social Reformer of the First Century AD*, by G.R.S. Mead, 1901 Edition

Ashtavakra Gita excerpts

Ashravaka Gita is one of the most important spiritual books which from the beginning speaks of the truth and of Self-realization. It carries the Teachings which Sage Ashtavakra gave to King Janak and, by the end of the teachings, King Janaka realized the Truth.

Here are selected excerpts from it on Self-Realization

Janaka said:

1.1

Master,

how is Knowledge to be achieved,

detachment acquired,

liberation attained?

Ashtavakra said:

1.2

To be free,

shun the experiences of the senses

like poison.

Turn your attention to

forgiveness, sincerity, kindness, simplicity, truth.

1.3

You are not earth, water, fire or air.

Nor are you empty space.

Liberation is to know yourself

as Awareness alone—

the Witness of these.

1.4

Abide in Awareness

with no illusion of person.

You will be instantly free and at peace.

1.5

You have no caste or duties.

You are invisible, unattached, formless.

You are the Witness of all things.

Be happy.

1.6

Right and wrong, pleasure and pain,

exist in mind only.

They are not your concern.

You neither do nor enjoy.

You are free.

1.7

You are the Solitary Witness

of All That Is,

forever free.

Your only bondage is not seeing This.

1.8

The thought: "I am the doer"

is the bite of a poisonous snake.

To know: "I do nothing"

is the wisdom of faith.

Be happy.

1.9

A single understanding:

"I am the One Awareness,"

consumes all suffering

in the fire of an instant.

Be happy.

1.10

You are unbounded Awareness—

Bliss, Supreme Bliss--

in which the universe appears

like the mirage of a snake in a rope.

Be happy.

1.11

It is true what they say:

"You are what you think."

If you think you are bound you are bound.

If you think you are free you are free.

1.12

You are Self—the Solitary Witness.

You are perfect, all-pervading, One.

You are free, desireless, forever still.

The universe is but a seeming in You.

1.13

Meditate on this: "I am Awareness alone--Unity itself."

Give up the idea that you are separate, a person,

that there is within and without.

1.14

You have long been bound thinking:

"I am a person."

Let the knowledge: "I am Awareness alone"

be the sword that frees you.

1.15

You are now and forever

free, luminous, transparent, still.

The practice of meditation

keeps one in bondage.

1.16

You are pure Consciousness—

the substance of the universe.

The universe exists within you.

Don't be small-minded.

1.17

You are unconditioned, changeless, formless.

You are solid, unfathomable, cool.

Desire nothing.

You are Consciousness.

1.18

That which has form is not real.

Only the formless is permanent.

Once this is known,

you will not return to illusion.

1.19

Just as a mirror exists

both within and without

the image reflected,

the Supreme Self exists

both within and without the body.

1.20

Just as the same space exists

both within and without a jar,

the timeless, all-pervasive One

exists as Totality.

Confirming Wisdom from A Course in Miracles

A Course in Miracles is a 3-volume modern phenomenon made up of a Text (T), a Workbook with 365 lesssons (W), and a Manual for Teachers (M).

Its teachings have remarkable parallels to the those offered in Vedic literature, including from such jewels as the **Upanishads** and the **Bhagavad Gita**, as well as to what is found in the wisdom of both Buddhists and Sufis.

These parallels may not be apparent immediately because the Course is expressed in Christian terminology.

Its basic message is that humans believe themselves to be separate from God. This separation extends to people's belief that they are individuals separate from others in the world.

It notes that our minds' mistaken thoughts and beliefs have assumed a lead role, identifying with the individual ego and taking over the position rightfully belonging to our true identity as Divine awareness. Our egos believe we are bound in bodies which are effectively prisons that gradually disintegrate and have an ending. Hence, as separate individuals, we suffer under a constant fear of eventual death.

The perceptions from the physical senses in our 'separate' bodies have created the world, time, and space as real, but the Course says the world of our waking state is really illusory and no different than dreams we have when sleeping. It points out that the Bible says Adam fell into a deep sleep but does not say anywhere later that he woke up (T, 2.3.6).

The purpose of the Course is to help us awaken from these illusions and waking dreams, beginning with transforming the nightmares and suffering our lives often are into happy dreams.

The reality which we can awaken to is peace and being one with God, changeless and eternal, outside of time and space, and without forms or names.

The Course speaks of correcting, or undoing, our mistaken beliefs and judgments that result in a sense of separation and bind and limit us. Accordingly, much of the Course's teaching and practice focuses on healing relationships, especially through forgiveness. Healing these misperceptions results in increased union because healing means 'making whole'.

This correction of perceptions and beliefs is what the Course means by a 'miracle'. This work is internal rather than a fixing of what is outside of us.

Time, as we experience it in the world, is to be used for this healing.

As we change our beliefs, so does our reality change. Mistaken beliefs can be likened to clouds blocking the reality of the sun from penetrating down to us. As we heal, so do the clouds thin and clear, bringing light to brighten our world and lives.

Forgiveness, as used by the Course, is not about a 'good me' forgiving a 'bad other', but just about correcting our own misjudgements and mistaken illusory concepts. As we make these internal shifts, forgiving ourselves for the errors we have made, our world and our experience of it also changes.

True joining with others results in what the Course calls 'holy relationship', leading to becoming the one Self and coming 'Home'.

When asked how many teachers of God are required (M, 12), the answer is one wholly perfect completed teacher who is therefore the Self and Son of God.

This atonement healing process is referred to as a 'journey without distance', as it is really just a recognition of the reality that is already present but which we have forgotten.

Some of the terminology ACIM uses compared to other teachings:

Separation = Belief in duality

Desire and resistance = both reinforce a sense of separation with what is desired or resisted

The peace of letting go = Relinquishing attachment

Joining = Yoga/union

Salvation = Enlightenment/samadhi

Atonement = 'at-one-ment', Oneness/Advaita

Indivisible = Oneness

Jesus Christ/'Older Brother' = Fully enlightened master/teacher/guru, our inner teacher/soul/atma

Holy Spirit/Voice for God = Inspiration (from the Divine) we open to when 'we' as egos get out of our own way

Kingdom of Heaven = Awareness senior to the mind

The Mystery of the Two Creations in Genesis

Genesis is the first of the five books in the Jewish Torah and the first book in the Christian Old Testament. Tradition has it that it was written by Moses. It far predates the time of Jesus.

Genesis tells the story of the origin of the world, of the heavens and of man. A puzzling aspect is that it speaks of God making the creation twice. The first creation is described in Genesis 1:1 to 2:3. The second creation begins at 2:4 and continues indefinitely.

Here are a few key differences between the two creations:

- The first creation took place over six days following which God rested on the seventh (1:1 – 2:3), while the second speaks of 'the day' in which the Lord God made the heavens and the earth (2:4).
- In the first creation God made man in his own image, making him male and female (1:27). In the second, God formed man from the dust of the ground and breathed life into him, so he became a living soul (2:7). Later He causes this first man, Adam, to fall asleep and takes a rib from him to use in forming the first woman, who is later named Eve (2:21 – 22).
- In the first creation, God gives man dominion over everything living thing that moves and over everything upon the face of the earth, including the fruit of every tree (1:28 – 29). In the second, God plants the garden of Eden and places man there, telling him he could eat the fruit of every tree except the fruit of the tree of knowledge of good and evil, saying he would surely die if he ate that (2:8 – 17).
- In the first creation no names are mentioned as being used for the living creatures or the plant life, but God requires man to name these in the second creation (2:19 – 20). Even man, as Adam and Eve, have names in the second creation but not in

the first. Furthermore, the garden and the rivers in it are given names in the second creation.

In the first creation, man – both male and female – is created in God's image. If one considers words like 'awareness' or 'love' to be what God is, then man as awareness or love would be in the image of God. Both these words – outside of time and space – have no boundaries, so the awareness and love of man would be one with the awareness and love that God is.

In the second creation, man is formed from the dust of the ground and, after God breathes life into him, man becomes a living soul. This suggests that such a soul, associated with a body made from the earth but quickened with God's breath, might still be divine but, as a mixture of the Divine and the physical, is now one remove from God.

In the first creation God declares it as good no less than seven times. In the last of these times, when observing everything He saw, He even says it is *very* good. The second creation not only has no such declaration but includes a tree of the knowledge of good and evil. So, in the first creation, no distinction is made between anything because everything is good. Distinguishing between things – good or bad, like or dislike – is a characteristic of the mind and personality.

The requirement of names is an aspect of the mind. A newborn baby knows no names, but has to be taught them all – and, of course, these vary according to culture and language.

The first creation does not have a mind – including personality and ego – as part of the Divine image of God that man – male and female – is, but the second one in manifested physical reality does.

The seven days of the first creation is significant in the sense that the very first days of a newly born infant are those in which it is not aware of itself as an individual being. It is not aware of having a body or a mind, but it is aware, and it certainly responds to love and instinctive physical needs. Such a newborn is still not only one with its mother but also still one with the Divine . . . but this oneness is in the realm of love and awareness, rather than in the realm of the physical or mental. Saying 4a in the *Gospel of Thomas* speaks being able to learn the place of life from a seven-day old baby.

Nowhere is it said that the first creation ever ceased to be, so it must be assumed still to be here, underlying the second creation and the world we live in today. In the *Gospel of Thomas* saying 113, Jesus is asked when the Kingdom is coming. He responds, 'the Kingdom of the Father is already spread out on the earth and people aren't aware of it.'

Accordingly, the Kingdom of Heaven is present with us now, but while we are focused on the second creation's world of objects, or names, and the mind's likes and dislikes, or good and evil, we have lost our connection with it.

Also, although Adam was put into a sleep in the second creation so that a rib could be taken from him to form woman, nowhere is it said he woke up. Presumably the second creation continues indefinitely with Adam remaining asleep to his real self in God's image, still present as the first creation . . .

Glossaries

Word meanings vary by teacher and tradition.

These definitions and clarifications reflect intended word usage in this book.

English words

Awareness – When pure it is the oneness of our true self, which is not personal, so not one's own awareness, but simply awareness without any reflection (duality) or action. When mental it is felt to be personal and is diluted through requiring reflections from what one perceives as objective, and it is therefore caught in duality.

Causal body – The seed body from which the physical and mental bodies emerge. Causal body is the beginning of the imagined separate individual.

Consciousness – The first move outward from oneness or the Source. Consciousness is then the intelligence and creator of manifested reality and is also the source of intelligent awareness, or the mind, of human beings, allowing them to be aware of the seen manifested creation, but also giving them the doorway back to their Source if they wish to seek that.

Ego – An illusory self, or mental 'I-ness', which believes it can manage one's worldly life. By assuming this control position, it blocks the true Self (Reality), so can be equated to ignorance and forgetfulness.

Gross body – The physical body which the subtle or mental body causes to act and react.

Insentient – That which is considered to be inanimate in the material realms.

Intellect – A discriminating faculty, the highest part of the mind which can be used by the seeker to move towards pure awareness.

Meditation – A state in which one has withdrawn from the mind and senses, and in which one is beyond the dimensions of time and space. One **IS** the meditation, rather than being the one – a human being – doing meditation.

Mind – An imaginary self which only functions when in relationship with something objective, be that a perception, thought or emotion. As this involves subject and object, mental awareness and mental intelligence exist in duality and are not pure awareness or pure intelligence. Identification with the mind is the experience of the waking state, which is forgetfulness and ignorance of one's Self or Home.

Sentient – The animate in the material realms, including human beings

Subtle body – The mental self (see Mind) which makes the gross or physical body act and react.

Witness – One's essential subjective Self, Knower, Observer, which is not only aware of itself, but aware of everything objective in its experience. This core Witness or Knower can also be thought of as one's centre. While it is aware of itself and everything else, nothing else, nothing lesser, including the mind, can be aware of it.

Sanskrit/Hindi words

Advaita – Nonduality

Ahamkara – Ego, the mind's 'I am'.

Antahkarana – Inner mind, the source from which the mind originates

Atma/Atman – Soul, spirit or one's essential self

Brahman – Ultimate reality, the absolute, or the highest universal principle which is without any individual thought

Buddhi – Intellect or discriminating part of the mind which makes decisions on what it receives from the manas in the form of perceptions, thoughts and emotions.

Chitta – Mental or subtle body

Dhyana – the state of withdrawal from the mind, senses and all externals to be one with one's Centre within, a heightened state, sometimes called samadhi or turiya, beyond the mind and dimensions of time and space.

Jagrat-sushupti – a state of continuous peace, like that found in deep dreamless sleep, but here it is with awareness so everyday life activities can continue to be carried out.

Jnani – One who is wise, learned, knowledgeable. May also mean one who is self-realized.

Karma – Action, work, deeds and karma also refers to the cause-and-effect principle by which one's intent and actions will result in future consequences of a similar nature.

Manas – Aspect of the mind which thinks, imagines, and receives perceptions or sensory inputs from the external.

Maya – Illusion, what is made of imagination, appearance we mistake for reality. Vedic literature speaks of the material realm being maya. Mind and ego are also maya. The illusion of maya tempts the mind and senses like a mirage tempts a person in the desert.

Mukti – Liberation

Rajas – One of three gunas – tamas, rajas and sattva – which in various combinations make up all of manifested reality. Rajas is passion, activity and movement.

Sahaja nirvikalpa samadhi – Absorption in oneself without mind or concepts, which is a state a yogi can continue to be in even while engaged in worldly activities.

Samadhi – Another word for union with the Divine, outside of the mind, time and space. The experience of such union is free from suffering, so of bliss or great peace.

Satsang – Being in the company of the highest truth.

Sattva – One of three gunas – tamas, rajas and sattva – which in various combinations make up all of manifested reality. Sattva or sattwa is harmony, calm and goodness.

Siddhi – Some level of spiritual attainment, often used to denote special powers, though these can distract one from one's further progress.

Tamas – One of three gunas – tamas, rajas and sattva – which in various combinations make up all of manifested reality. Tamas is ignorance, inertia and laziness.

Turiya – Often referred to the 'fourth state' to distinguish it from the three states known to human beings of waking, dreaming and deep dreamless sleep, turiya would better be understood as the original and permanent state which underlies and is present with all the other states. Turiya is a state of pure awareness senior to, and independent of, the mind, senses, personality and ego. As it is a state of oneness, it is also a state of yoga or union.

Vasanas – Desires and wishes, sub-conscious or unconscious tendencies, the impulses and drivers, we bring into this life at birth. Vasanas are always caught in the imaginary world of duality.

Vedas/Vedic teachings and philosophy – A large body of spiritual knowledge originating in ancient India and written in Sanskrit which forms the basis of Hindu religion. Some of the Vedas, like the Upanishads, are the first written records teaching how to realize God or the Self.

Viraha – Separation from, absence of.

Vrittis – Thoughts which are likened to waves or whirlpools disturbing the calm of the oceanic Self. Each vritti is separate from the Self and therefore existing in the ignorance of duality.

Yoga – Union or oneness with the Divine. An end to duality of all subject and object relationships and the cessation of manifested reality.

Acknowledgements

A debt is owed to too many for them all to be named here. With profound gratitude, I bow down to all of them as emissaries of the One Source.

Diagrams from headless.org are included with Richard Lang's kind permission.

The 'Traditions' section of headless.org has been a great help in selecting a number of the excerpts from teachers and traditions, as was Richard Lang's 1998 '*Seeing Who You Really Are*' Spiritweb Online Class and the booklet *On Being One-Self – A Resource Book of Modern Experiments and Traditional Wisdom*, edited by Anne Seward and published by Shollond Publications.

The following teachers and teachings have made major contributions to the author's understanding, practice and experience expressed in this booklet.

A Course in Miracles

Aitken Roshi, Robert – Gateless Barrier – The Wu-men Kuan (Mumonkan)

Arka, Srinivas – Talks, Adventures in Self-Discovery, Becoming Inspired

Bhagavad Gita

Blofeld, John - Taoism – The Road to/Quest for Immortality

Gospel of Thomas, translation by Stevan Davies

Gurdjieff, George – In Search of the Miraculous (by P. D. Ouspensky)

Hamilton, Helen – Dissolving the Ego, Reality Check

Harding, Douglas – The Hierarchy of Heaven and Earth, The Little Book of Life and Death

Norbu, Namkai – The Mirror – Advice on the Presence of Awareness

Nisargadatta – Dialogues, The Experience of Nothingness

Patanjali Yoga Sutras

Pilgrim, A. – Awake – Conscious Pilgrimage

Ramana Maharshi – Dialogues, The Collected Works of

Ramana Maharshi, Conscious Immortality

Siddharameshwar Maharaj – Master Key to Self-Realization

Shyam, Swami – Satsang talks, Bhagavad Gita, Brahm Jyoti – 9 Upanishads

Spezzano, Chuck and Lency – Workshops, Psychology of Vision's Triangle Journey Model

Upanishads (Principal)

Warren, Shaun de – Prosperity Club talks, You Are the Key, The Mirror of Life

Index

WHO AM I ?

An exploration of our essential nature

B E Mayne

Based on the author's own understanding and experience.

Derived from decades of work with numerous teachers and teachings.

Supportive and confirming quotes from teachers and traditions throughout history.

- Robert Aitken Roshi
- Srinivas Arka
- Bhagavad Gita
- John Blofeld
- The Gateless Barrier - Mumonkan
- Douglas Harding
- Namkai Norbu
- Nisargadatta
- Patanjali Yoga Sutras
- Ramana Maharshi
- Shaun de Warren
- Siddharameshwar Maharaj
- Swami Shyam
- Principal Upanishads

Printed in Great Britain
by Amazon

44995144R00078